THE INCREDIBLE HISTORY OF THE VEDIC PERIOD!

GOLU KUMAR

Copyright © Golu Kumar
All Rights Reserved.

This book has been published with all efforts taken to make the material error-free after the consent of the author. However, the author and the publisher do not assume and hereby disclaim any liability to any party for any loss, damage, or disruption caused by errors or omissions, whether such errors or omissions result from negligence, accident, or any other cause.

While every effort has been made to avoid any mistake or omission, this publication is being sold on the condition and understanding that neither the author nor the publishers or printers would be liable in any manner to any person by reason of any mistake or omission in this publication or for any action taken or omitted to be taken or advice rendered or accepted on the basis of this work. For any defect in printing or binding the publishers will be liable only to replace the defective copy by another copy of this work then available.

Contents

CHAPTER ONE

THE VDIC PERIOD

Let us imagine we are in a village of an Aryan tribe in the Eastern Panjab something more than thirty centuries ago. It is made up of a few large huts, around which clusters smaller ones, all of them rudely built, mostly of bamboo; in the other larger ones dwell the heads of families, while the smaller ones shelter their kinsfolk and followers, for this is a patriarchal world, and the housefather gives the law to his household. The people are mostly a comely folk, tall and clean-limbed, and rather fair of skin, with well-cut features and straight noses; but among them are not a few squats and ugly men and women, flat-nosed and nearly black, color once the free dwellers in this land, and now have become slaves or serfs to their Aryan conquerors. Around the village are fields where bullocks are dragging rough plows and beyond these are woods and moors in which lurk wild men, and beyond these are the lands of other Aryan tribes. Life in the village is simple and rude, but not uneventful, for the village is part of a tribe, and tribes are constantly fighting with one another, as well as with the dark-skinned men who often try to drive back the Aryans, sometimes in small forays and sometimes in massed hordes. But the world in which the village is interested is a small one, and hardly extends beyond the bounds of the land where its tribe dwells. It knows something of the land of the Five Rivers, in one corner of which it lives, and something even of the lands to the north of it, and to the west as far as the mountains and deserts, where live men of its kind and tongue; but beyond these limits, it, does not know. Only a few bold spirits have traveled eastward across the high slope that divides the land of the Five Rivers from the strange and mysterious countries around the great rivers Gaṅgā and Yamunā, the unknown land of deep forests and swarming dark-skinned men.

In the matter of religion, these Aryans care a good deal about charms and spells, black and white magic, preventing or curing all kinds of diseases or mishaps, winning success in love and war and trade and husbandry, for bringing harm upon enemies or rivals--charms which a few centuries later will be dressed up in Ṛigvēdic style, stuffed out with imitations of Ṛigvēdic hymns, and published under the name of Atharva vēda, "the lore of the Atharvans," by wizards who claim to belong to the old priestly clans of Atharvan and Aṅgiras. But we have not yet come so far, and as yet all that these people can tell us is a great deal about their black and white magic, in which they are hugely interested, and a fair amount about certain valiant men of olden times who are now worshipped by them as helpful spirits, and a little about some vague spirits who are in the sun and the air and the fire and other places, and are very high and great but are not interesting at all.

This popular religion seems to be a hopeless one, without ideals and symbols of love and hope. Is there nothing better to be found in this place? Yes, there is a priestly religion also; and if we would know something about it we must listen to the chanting of the priests, the _brahmans_ or men of the "holy spirit," as they are called, who are holding a sacrifice now on behalf of the rich lord who lives in the largest house in the village--a service for which they expect to be paid with a handsome fee of oxen and gold. They are priests by heredity, wise in the knowledge of the ways of the gods; some of them understand how to compose _riks_, or hymns, in the fine speech dear to their order, hymns which are almost sure to win the gods' favor, and all of them know how the sacrifices shall be performed with perfect exactness so that no slip or imperfection may mar their efficacy. Their psalms are called _Rig-vēda_, "lore of the verses," and they set themselves to find grace in the ears of the many gods whom these priests worship, sometimes by open praise and sometimes by riddling description of the exploits and nature of the gods. Often they are very fine, but always they are the work of priests, and artists in ritual. And if you look heedfully into it you will also mark that these priests are inclined to think that the act of sacrifice, the offering of, say, certain oblations in a particular manner with particular words accompanying them, is in itself potent, quite apart from the psalms which they sing over it, that it has a magic power of its own over the machinery of nature.[1] This is no new idea of our Vēdic priests; ten thousand years before them their remote forefathers believed it and acted upon it, and if for example, they wanted rain they would sprinkle drops of water and utters magic words. Our Vēdic priests have now different kinds of symbols, but all the same, they still have the notion that ceremony, _rita_ as they call it, has a magic potency of its own. Let us mark this well, for we shall see much issuing from it.

Who are the gods to whom these priests offer their prayers and psalms? They are many, and of various kinds. Most of them are taken from the religion of the people and dressed in new garb according to the imagination of the pries, and a few are priestly inventions altogether. There is Dyaush-pitā, the Sky-father, with Pṛithivī Mātā, the Earth-mother; there are Vāyu the Wind-spirit, Parjanya the Rain-god, Sūrya the Sun-god, and other spirits of the sky such as Savitā; there is the Dawn-goddess, Ushās. All these are or were originally deified powers of nature: the people, though their imagination created them, have never felt any deep interest in them, and the priests who have taken them into their charge, though they treat them very courteously and sing to them elegant hymns full of figures of speech, have not been able to cover them with the flesh and blood of living personality. Then we have Agni the Fire-god, and Sōma the spirit of the intoxicating juice of the sōma-plant, which is used to inspire the pious to drunken raptures in certain ceremonies; both of these have acquired particular importance through their association with priestly worship, especially Agni, because he, as bearing to the gods the sacrifices cast into his flames, has become the ideal Priest and divine Paraclete of Heaven. Nevertheless, ss all this hieratic importance has not made them gods in the deeper sense, reigning in the hearts of men. Then we find powers of doubtful origin, Mitra and Varuṇa and Vishṇu and Rudra, and figures of heroic legend, like the warrior Indra and the twin charioteers called Aśvinaā and Nāsatyā. All these, with many others, have their worship in the Ṛig-vēda: the priests sing their praises lustily, and often speak now of one deity, now of another, as being the highest divinity, without the least consistency.

Some savage races believe in the highest god or first divine Being in whom they feel little personal interest. They seldom speak of him, and hardly ever worship him. So it seems to be with Dyaush-pitā. The priests speak of him and to him, but only in connexion with other gods; he has not a single whole hymn in his honor, and the only definite attribute that attaches to him is that of fatherhood. Yet he has become a great god among other races akin in a speech to the Aryans of India: Dyaush-pitā is phonetically the same as the Greek [Greek: Zeus patêr] and the Latin _Iuppiter_. How comes it then that he is not, and never was, a god in the true sense among the Indian Aryans? Because, I think, his name has always betrayed him. To call a deity "Sky-father" is to label him as a mere abstraction. No mystery, no possibility of human personality, can gather around those two plain prose words. So long as a deity is known by the name of the physical agency that he represents, so long will he be unable to grow into a personal God in India. The priests may sing vociferous psalms to Vāyu the Wind-spirit and Sūrya the Sun-spirit, and even to their beloved Agni the Fire-god; but sing as much as they will, they never can make the people, in general, take them to their hearts.

Observe what a different history is that of Zeus among the Greeks--Zeus, Father of Gods and Men, the ideal of kingly majesty and wisdom and goodness. The reason is patent. Ages and ages before the days when the Homeric poets sang, the Greeks had forgotten that Zeus originally meant "sky": it had become to them a personal name of a great spiritual power, which they were free to invest with the noblest ideal of personality. But very likely there is also another reason: I believe that the Olympian Zeus, as modeled by Homer and accepted by following generations, was not the original [Greek: _Zeus patêr_] at all, but a usurper who had robbed the old Sky-father of his throne and his title as well, that he was at the outset a hero-king who somsometimeter his death was raised to the seat and dignity of the old Sky-father and received likewise his name. This theory explains the old hero-sagas which are connected with Zeus and the strange fact that the Cretans pointed to a spot on their island where they believed Zeus was buried. It explains why legends persistently averred that Zeus expelled his father Kronos from the throne and suppressed the Titan dynasty: on my view, Kronos was the original Father Zeus, and his name of Zeus and rank as a chief god were appropriated by a deified hero. How natural such a process was in those days may be seen from the liturgy of Unas's on the pyramids at Sakkara in Egypt.[2] Here Unas's is described as rising in heaven after his death as a supreme god, devouring his fathers and mothers, slaughtering the gods, eating their "magical powers," and swallowing their "spirit-souls," so that he thus becomes "the first-born of the first-born gods," omniscient, omnipotent, and eternal, identified with the Osiris, the highest god. Now, this Unas's was a real historical man; he was the last king of the Fifth Dynasty and was deified after death, just like any other king of Egypt. The early Egyptians, like many savage tribes, regarded all their kings as gods on earth and paid them formal worship after their death; the later Egyptians, going a step further, worshipped them even in their lifetime as embodiments of the gods.[3] What is said in the liturgy for the deification of Unas's is much the same as was said of other kings. The dead king in early Egypt becomes a god, even the greatest of the gods, and he assumes the name of that god[4]; he overcomes the other gods by brute force, hand-e killing, and devours them. This is very like what I think was the case with Zeus; the main difference is that in Egypt the _character_ of the deified king was merged with that of the old god, and men continued to regard the latter in the same light as before; but among the forefathers of the Greeks the reverse happened in at least one case, that of Zeus, where the character of a hero who had peculiarly fascinated popular imagination partly eclipsed that of the old god whose name and rank he usurped. The reason for this, I suppose, is that even the early Egyptians had already a conservative religion with fixed traditions and a priesthood that forgot nothing,[5] whereas, among the forefathers of the Greeks, who were wandering savages, social order and religion were in a very fluid state. However that may be, a deified hero might oust an older god and reign under his name; and this theory explains many difficulties in the legends of Zeus.

As to the Roman Iuppiter, I need not say much about him. Like all the genuine gods of Latium, he never was much more than an abstraction until the Greeks came with their literature and dressed him in the wardrobe of their Zeus.

Coming now to Ushās, the Lady of the Dawn, and looking at her name from the standpoint of comparative philosophy, we see that the word _ushās_ is closely connected with the Greek [Greek: heôs] and the Latin _aurora_. But when we read the literature, we are astonished to find that while the Greek Dawn-lady has remained almost always a mere abstraction, the Indian spirit is a lovely, living woman instinct with the richest sensuous charms of the East. Some twenty hymns are addressed to her, and for the most part, they are alive with real poetry, with a sense of beauty and gladness and sometimes withal an under-note of sadness for the brief joys of life. But when we look carefully into it we notice a curious thing: all this hymn-singing to Ushās is purely literary and artistic, and there is practically no religion at all at the back of it. A few stories are told of her, but they seem to convince no one, and she certainly has no ritual worship apart from these hymns, which are poetical essays more than anything else. The priestly poets are thrilled with sincere emotion at the sight of the dawn, and are inspired by it to stately and lively descriptions of its beauties and to touching reflections upon the passing of time and mortal life; but in this scene, Ushās herself is hardly more than a model from an artist's studio, in a very Bohemian quarter. More than once on account of the free display of her charms she is compared to a dancing girl or even a common harlot! Here the imagination is at work which in course of time will populate the Hindu Paradise with a celestial _corps de ballet_, the fair and frail Apsarasas. Our Vēdic Ushās is a forerunner of that gay company. A charming person, indeed; but certainly no genuine goddess.

As his name shows, Sūrya is the spirit of the sun. We hear a good deal about him in the Rig-vēda, but the whole of it is merely a description of the power of the sun in the order of nature, partly allegorical, and partly literal. He is only a nature-power, not a personal god. The case is not quite so clear with Savitā, whose name seems to mean literally "stimulator," "one who stirs up." On the whole, it seems most likely that he represents the sun, as the vivifying power in nature, though some[6] think that he was originally an abstraction of the vivifying forces in the world and later became connected with the sun. However this may be, Savitā is and remains an impersonal spirit with no human element in his character.

Still more perplexing are the two deities Mitra and Varuṇa, who are very often associated with one another, and are related. Mitra certainly is an old god: if we go over the mountains to the west and north-west of the country of our Indian Aryans, we shall find their kinsmen in Persia and Bactria worshipping him as a power that maintains the laws of righteousness and guards the sanctity of oaths and engagements, who by means fusing keeps mankind under his observation and with his terrible weapons crushes evil powers. The Indian Aryans tell almost the same tale of their Mitra and his companion Varuṇa, who perhaps is simply a doublet of Mitra with a different name, which perhaps is due to a variety of worship. But they have more to say of Varuṇa than of Mitra. In Varuṇa, we have the highest ideal of spirituality that the Hindu religion will reach for many centuries. Not only is he described as the supreme controller of the order of nature--that is an attribute which these priestly poets ascribe with generous inconsistency to many others of their deities--but he is likewise the omniscient guardian of the moral law and the rule of religion, sternly punishing sin and falsehood with his dreaded noose, but showing mercy to the penitent and graciously communing with the sage who has found favor in his eyes.

But Mitra and Varuṇa will not enjoy this exalted rank for long. Soon the priests will declare that Mitra rules over the day and Varuṇa over the night (TS. II. i. 7, 4; VI. iv. 8, 3), and then Varuṇa will begin to sink in honor. The "noose of

Varuṇa" will come to mean merely the disease of dropsy. His connection with the darkness of the night will cause men to think of him with fear; and in their dread, they will forget his ancient attributes of universal righteousness, justice, and mercy, and remember him chiefly as an avenger of guilt. They will banish him to the distant seas, whose rivers he now guides over the earth in his gracious government of nature; and there he will dwell in exile forever, remembered only to be feared. And Mitra will become merely another name for the sun.

What is the origin of this singular couple? And why are they destined to this fall? Neither of these questions can be answered by anything but conjectures. There is no evidence either from Indian or Iranian religion that Mitra or his double Varuṇa grew out of the worship of the sun or the sky, although in their worship they were sometimes connected with the sun and the sky. However far back we look, we still find them essentially spirits of natural order and moral law, gods in the higher sense of the word. But their character, and especially the character of Varuṇa, it seems to me, is rather too high to survive the competition of rival cults, such as that of the popular hero Indra and the priests' darling Agni, which tend to engross the interest of worshippers lay and cleric, and to blunt their relish for more spiritual ideals. So Mitra and Varuṇa become stunted in their growth; and, a times e fatal time when they are identified with the sky by day and night. This is the final blow. No deity that is limited to any one phase or form of nature in India can be or become a great god, and speedily all their real divinity fades away from Mitra and Varuṇa, and they shrivel into insignificance.

Next, we turn to a spirit of a very different sort, the Fire-god, Agni. The word _agni_ is identical to the Latin _ignis_; it means "fire," and nothing else but fire, and this fact is quite sufficient to prevent Agni from becoming a great god. The priests indeed do their best, by fertile fancy and endless repetition of his praises, to lift him to that rank; but even they cannot do it. From the days of the earliest generations of men Fire was a spirit; and the household fire, which cooks the food of the family and receives its simple oblations of clarified butter, is a kindly genius of the home. But with all his usefulness and elfish mystery Fire simply remains fire, and there's an end to it, for the ordinary man. But the priests will not have it so. The chief concern of their lives is with sacrifice, and their deepest interest is in the spirit of the sacrificial fire. All the riches of their imagination and their vocabulary are lavished upon him, his forms, and his activities. They have devoted to him about 200 hymns and many occasional verses, in which they dwell with constant delight and ingenious metaphor upon his splendor, his power, his birth from wood, from the two firesticks, from trees of the forest, from stones, or as lightning from the clouds, his kinship with the sun, his dwelling in three abodes (viz. as a rule on earth, in the clouds as lightning, and the upper heavens as the sun), his place in the homes of men as a holy guest, a friend and a kinsman, his protection of worshippers against evil spirits and malignant sorcerers, and especially his function of conveying the oblation poured into his flames up to the gods. Thus they are led to represent him as the divine Priest, the ideal hierophant, in whom are united the functions of the three chief classes of Ṛigvēdic sacrificial priests, the _hōtā_, _adhvaryu_, and _brahman_, and hence as an all-knowing sage and seer. If infinite zeal and ingenuity in singing Agni's praises and glorifying his activities can avail to raise him to the rank of a great god, we may expect to find him very near the top. But it is not to be. The priests cannot convince the plain man of Agni's super-godhead, and soon they will fail to convince even themselves. The time will shortly come when they will regard all these gods as little more than puppets whose strings are pulled by the mysterious spirit of the sacrifice.

The priests have another pet deity, Sōma. ForThecred rites include the pressing and drinking of the fermented yellow juice of the sōma-plant, an acid draught with intoxicating powers, which when mixed with milk and drunk in the priestly rites inspires religious ecstasy. This drinking of the sōma-juice is already an ancient and important feature in the worship of our Aryans, as it is also among their kinsmen in Iran; so it is no wonder that the spirit of the sacred plant has been made by the priests into an important deity and celebrated with an endless abundance of praise and prayer. As with Agni, Sōma's appearance and properties are described with an inexhaustible wealth of epithets and metaphors. The poets love to dwell on the mystic powers of this wonderful potion, which can heal the sickness of soul and body and inspire gods and men to mighty deeds and holy ecstasy. Most often they tell how the god Indra drank huge potions of it to strengthen himself for his great fight with the dragon Vṛitra. Most of this worship is of the priestly invention; voluminous as its rhetoric is, it makes no great impression on the laity, nor perhaps on the clergy either. Some of the more ingenious the priests are already beginning to trace an affinity between Sōma and the moon.

The yellow sōma-stalks swell in the water of the pressing-vat, as the yellow moon waxes in the sky; the _soma_ has a magical power of stimulation, and the moon sends forth a mystic liquid influence over the vegetation of the earth, and especially over magic plants; the sōma is a rosia drunk by gods and heroes to inspire them to mighty deeds, and the moon is a bowl of ambrosia which is periodically drunk by the gods and therefore wanes month by month. The next step will soon be taken, and the priests will say that Sōma _is_ the moon, and literature will then obediently accept this statement, and, gradually forgetting nearly everything that Sōma meant to the Ṛigvēdic priests, will use the name Sōma merely as a secondary name for Chandra, the moon and its god. A very illuminating process, which shows how a god may utterly change his nature. Now we turn to the hero-gods.

Indra and the Aśvinā at the beginning came to be worshipped because they were heroes, men who were supposed to have wrought marvelously noble and valiant deeds in dim far-off days, saviors of the afflicted, champions of the right, and who for this reason were worshipped after death, perhaps even before death, as divine beings, and gradually became associated in their legends and the forms of their worship with all kinds of other gods. Times change, gods grow old and fade away, but the remembrance of great deeds lives on in strange wild legends, which, however much they may borrow from other worships and however much they may be obscured by the phantom lights of false fancy, still throw a glimmer of true light back through the darkness of the ages into an immeasurably distant past.

Indra is a mighty giant, tawny of hair and beard and tawny of aspect. The poets tell us that he bears up or stretches out earth and sky, even that he has created heaven and earth. He is a monarch supreme among the gods, the lord of all beings, immeasurable and irresistible in power. He rides in a golden chariot drawn by two tawny horses, or many horses, even as many as eleven hundred, and he bears as his chief weapon the _vajra_, or thunderbolt, sometimes also a bow with arrows, a hook, or a net. Of all drinkers of sōma, he is the lustiest; he swills many lakes of it, and he eats mightily of the flesh of bulls and buffaloes. To his worshippers, he gives an abundance of wealth and happiness, and he leads them to victory over hostile tribes of Aryans and the still more dreaded hordes of dark-skins, the Dāsas and Dasyus. He guided the prince's Yadu and Turvaśa across the rivers, he aided Divōdāsa Atithigva to discomfit the dark-skinned Śambara, he gave Divōdāsa's son Sudās the victory over the armies of the ten allied kings beside the river Parushṇī. Many are the names of the devils and demons that have fallen before him; but most glorious of all his deeds is the conquest of Vṛitra, the dragon dwelling in a mountain fastness amidst the waters, where Indra, accompanied by the troop of Maruts, or storm-gods, slew the monster with his bolt and set free the waters, or recovered the hidden kine. Our poets sing endless variations on this theme, ad sometimes speak of Indra repeating the exploit for the benefit of his worshippers, which is as much as to say that they, or at least some of them, think it an allegory.

In all this maze of savage fancy and priestly invention and wild exaggeration, some points stand out clearly. Indra is a god of the people, particularly of the fighting man, a glorified type of the fair-haired, hard-fighting, hard-drinking forefathers of the Indian Aryans and their distant cousins the Hellenes; therefore he is the champion of their armies in battles. He is not a fiction of hieratic imagination, whom priests regale with hyperbolic flattery qualified only by the lukewarmness of their belief in their own words. He is a living personality in the faith of the people; the priests only invent words to express the people's faith and perhaps add to the old legends some riddling fancies of their own. Many times they tell us that after conquering Vṛitra and setting free the waters or the kine Indra created the light, the dawn, or the sun; or they say that he produced them without mentioning any fight with Vṛitra; sometimes they speak of him as setting free "the kine of the Morning," which means that they understood the cows to signify the light of morning, and it would seem also that they thought that the waters mentioned in the story signified the rain. But why do they speak of these acts as heroic deeds, exploits of a mighty warrior, in the same tone and with the same epic fire as when they sing of Indra's battles in times near to their own, real battles in which their forefathers, strong in their faith in the god, shattered the armies of hostile Aryan tribes or the fortresses of dark-skinned natives? The personality of Indra and the spirit in which his deeds are recounted remind us of hero-sagas; the allegories which the poets read into them are on the other hand quite in the style of the priest. How can we explain the presence of these two voices? Besides, why should the setting free of the rain or the daylight be a peculiarly heroic attribute of Indra? Other gods are said to do the same things as part of their regular duties: Parjanya, Mitra and Varuṇa, Dyaus, dispense the rain, and others the light.

The explanation is simple. Indra, it seems to me, is a god of just the same sort as Zeus, whose nature and history I have already explained according to my lights. In the far-away past, Indra was simply a hero: very likely he was once a chieftain on earth. The story of his great deeds so fascinated the imagination of men that they worshipped his memory and at last raised him to the rank of a chief god. Now they had previously worshipped two very high gods; one of these was Dyaush-pitā, the Sky-father, of whom I have spoken before, and another was Tvashṭā, the All-creator. So some of them, as the Ṛig-vēda proves, declared that Dyaus was the father of Indra, and others appear to have given this honor to Tvashṭā, while others regarded Tvashṭā as Indra's grandfather; and some even said that to obtain the sōma to inspire him to divine deeds Indra killed his father, which of course is just an imaginative way of saying that Indra was made into a god and worshipped in place of the elder god.

The puzzle now is solved. Indra has remained down to the time of the Ṛig-vēda true to his early nature, an epic hero and typical warrior; but he has also borrowed from the old Sky-father the chief attributes of a sky-spirit, especially the giving of rain and the making of light, which the priests of the Ṛig-vēda riddlingly describe as setting free the waters and the cows. He bears the thunderbolt, as does also Zeus; like Zeus, he has got it from the Sky-father, who had likewise a thunderbolt, according to some Rigvēdic poets, though others say it was forged for him by Tvashṭā, his other father. I even venture to think that there is a kernel of heroic legend in the story of the slaying of Vṛitra; that at the bottom it is a tale relating how Indra with a band of brave fellows stormed a mountain hold surrounded by water in which dwelt a wicked chieftain who had carried away the cattle of his people, and that when Indra had risen to the rank of a great god of the sky men added to this plain tale much mythical decoration appropriate to his new quality, turning the comrades of Indra into the storm-gods and interpreting the waters and cows to mean rain and daylight. Since most of us are agreed that stories such as that of Indra defeating Śambara for the benefit of Divōdāsa refer to real events, it seems unnatural to suppose that the Vṛitra legend is a purely imaginary myth. We can thus explain why the ideas of Indra setting free the rain and the light fit in so awkwardly with the heroic element in the legend: for they are merely secondary attributes, borrowed from the myths of other gods and mechanically attached to Indra on his elevation in the pantheon. But we can explain much more. There is a regular cycle of hero-saga connected with Indra which is visible or half-visible at the back of some of the Vēdic hymns and of the priestly literature which is destined to follow them.

The truth is that the priests of the Ṛig-vēda on the whole have not quite made up their minds about Indra's merits, and we shall find them a few generations hence equally uncertain. They praise his heroic deeds lustily and admire his power immensely, but they are keenly aware that he is a god with a past, and sometimes they dwell on that. Their favorite method is to relate some of his former questionable deeds in the form of reproach, and then to turn the story to his credit in some way or another; but as time goes on and the priests think less and less of most of their gods, Indra's character will steadily sink, and in the end, we shall find him playing a subordinate part, a debauched king in a sensuous paradise, popularly worshipped as a giver of rain. But this is to anticipate. As yet Indra is to the Ṛigvēdic priests a very great god; but how did he become so? If we read carefully the hymn RV. IV. xviii.[7] we see at the back of it a story somewhat like this. Before he was born, Tvashṭā, Indra's grandfather, knew that Indra would dispossess him of his sovereignty over the gods, and therefore did his best to prevent his birth (cf. RV. III. xlviii.); but the baby Indra would not be denied, and he forced his way into the light of day through the side of his mother Aditi, who seems to be the same as Mother Earth (cf. _Ved. Stud._, ii, p. 86), killed his father, and drank Tvashṭā's sōma, by which he obtained divine powers. In v. 12 of this hymn, Indra excuses himself by saying that he was in great straits and that then the sōma was brought to him by an eagle. What these straits were is indicated in another hymn (IV. xxvii.), which tells us that he was imprisoned, and escaped on the back of the eagle, which he compelled to carry him; the watchman Kṛiśānu shot an arrow at the bird, but it passed harmlessly through its feathers. Evidently in the story, Indra had a hard struggle with rival gods. One poet says (RV. IV. xxx. 3): "Not even all the gods, O Indra, defeated thee when thou didst lengthen days into nights," which refers also to some miracle like that ascribed to Joshua. Another tradition (MS. I. vi. 12) relates that while Indra and his brother Vivasvān were still unborn they declared their resolve to oust the Ādityas, the elder sons of their mother Aditi; so the Ādityas tried to kill them when born and slew Vivasvān, but Indra escaped. Another version (TS. II. iv. 13) says that the gods, being afraid of Indra, bound him with fetters before he was born; and at the same time, Indra is, identified with the Rājanya, or warrior class, as its type and representative.[8] This last point is immensely important, for it clinches the matter. Not once, but repeatedly, the priestly literature of the generations that will follow immediately after that of the Ṛig-vēda will be found to treat Indra as the type of the war order. They will describe an imaginary coronation-ceremony of Indra, ending with these words: "Anointed with this great anointment Indra won all victories, found all the worlds, attained the superiority, pre-eminence, and supremacy over all the gods, and having won the overlordship, the paramount ruler, the self-rule, the sovereignty, the supreme authority, the kingship, the great kingship, the suzerainty in this world, self-existing, self-ruling, immortal, in yonder world of heaven, having attained all desires he became immortal." Thus we see that amidst the maze of obscure legends about Indra three points stand out with perfect clearness. They are, firstly, that Indra was a usurper; secondly, that the older gods fought hard but vainly to keep him from supreme divinity, and that in his struggle he killed his father; and thirdly, that he was identified with the warrior class, as opposed to the priestly order, or Brahmans. This antagonism to the Brahmans is brought out very clearly in some versions of the tales of his exploits. More than once the poets of the Ṛig-vēda hint that his slaying of Vṛitra involved some guilt, the guilt of _brahma-hatyā_, or slaughter of a being in whom the _brahma_, or holy spirit, was embodied; and this is explained clearly in a priestly tale (TS. II. v. 2, 1 ff.; cf. ŚB. I. i. 3, 4, vi. 3, 8), according to which Indra from jealousy killed Tvashṭā's son Viśvarūpa, who was chaplain of the gods, and thus he incurred the guilt of _brahma-hatyā_. Then Tvashṭā held a sōma-sacrifice; Indra, being excluded from it, broke up the ceremony and himself drank the sōma. The sōma that was left over Tvashṭā cast into one of the sacred fires and produced thereby from it the giant Vṛitra, by whom the whole universe, including Agni and Sōma, was enveloped (cf. the later version in Mahābhārata, V. viii. f.). By slaying him Indra again became guilty of _brahma-hatyā_, and some Ṛigvēdic poets hint that it was the consciousness of this sin that made him flee away after the deed was done.

These bits of the saga prove, as effectually as is possible in a case like this, that Indra was originally a warrior-king or chieftain who was deified, perhaps by the priestly tribe of the Aṅgirasas, who claim in some of the hymns to have aided him in his fight with Vṛitra, and that he thus rose to the first rank in the pantheon, gathering around himself a great cycle of heroic legend based upon those traditions, and only secondarily and by artificial invention becoming associated with the control of the rain and the daylight.

The name Aśvinā means "The Two Horsemen"; what their other name, Nāsatyā, signifies nobody has satisfactorily explained. But even with the name Aśvinā, there is a difficulty. They are described usually as riding together in a chariot which is sometimes said to be drawn by horses, and this would suit their name; but more often the poets say that their chariot is drawn by birds, such as eagles or swans, and sometimes even by a buffalo or buffaloes, or by an ass. I do not see how we can escape from this difficulty except by supposing that popular imagination regarding this matter varied from very early times, but preferred to think of them as having horses. At any rate, they are very ancient gods, for the people of Iran also have traditions about them, and in the far-away land of Mitanni, in the north of Mesopotamia, they are invoked together with Indra, Mitra, and Varuṇa to sanction treaties. In India the Aryans keep them very busy, for they are more than anything else gods of help. Thrice every day and thrice every night they sally forth on their patrols through earth and heaven, in oto the distressed: and the poets tell us the names of many persons whom they have relieved, such as old Chyavāna, whom they restored to youth and love, Bhujyu, whom they rescued from drowning in the ocean, Atri, whom they saved from a fiery pit, Viśpalā, to whom when her leg had been cut off they gave one of iron, and Ghōshā, to whom they brought a husband. Many other helpful acts are ascribed to them, and at least some of these stories are likely more or less true. Another legend relates that they jointly wedded Sūryā, the daughter of the Sun-god, who chose them from amongst the other gods.

CHAPTER TWO

Amidst the medley of saga and facts and poetical imagination which surrounds the Aśvinā, can we see the outlines of their original character? It is hard to say: opinions must differ. The Aryans of India are inclined to say that they are simply divine kings active in good works; but the priests are perhaps beginning to fancy that they may be embodiments of powers of nature--they are not sure which--and in course of time they will have various theories, partly connected with their rituals. But all that is certain in the Vēdic age about the Aśvins is that they are an ancient pair of savior-gods who ride about in a chariot and render constant services to mankind. We are tempted however to see a likeness between them and the [Greek: Diòs kórô] of the distant Hellenes, the heroes Kastor and Polydeukes, Castor and Pollux, the twin Horsemen who are saviors of afflicted mankind by land and sea. There are difficulties in the way of this theory, but they are not insurmountable, and I believe that the Aśvinā of India has the same origin as the Twin Horsemen of Greece. At any rate, both the pairs are hero-gods, whose divinity has been created by mankind's need for help and admiration for valor. Whether there was any human history at the back of this process we cannot say.

Now we may leave the heroes and consider a god of a very different kind, Vishṇu.

The Ṛig-vēda has not very much to say about Vishṇu, and what it says is puzzling. The poets figure him as a beneficent young giant, of unknown parentage, with two characteristic attributes: the first of these is his three mystic strides, and the second is his close association with Indra. Very often they refer to these three strides, sometimes using the verb _vi-kram_, "to step out," sometimes the adjectives _uru-krama_, "widely-stepping," and _uru-gāya_, "wide-going." The three steps carry Vishṇu across the three divisions of the universe, the highest of which is his home, which he shares with Indra (RV. I. xxxii. 20, clip. 5-6, III. lv. 10; cf. AB. I. i., etc.). Some of them are beginning to imagine that these steps symbolize the passage of the sun through the three divisions of the world, the earth, sky, and upper heaven; certainly, this idea will be held by many later scholars, though a few will maintain that it denotes the sun at its rising, at midday, and its setting. Before long we shall find some priests harping on the same notion in another form, saying that Vishṇu's head was cut off by accident and became the sun; and later on, we shall see Vishṇu bearing as one of his weapons a chakra, or discus, which looks like a figure of the sun. But all this is an afterthought: in the Vēda, and the priestly literature that follows directly upon the Vēda, Vishṇu is _not_ the sun. Nor do we learn what he is very readily from his second leading attribute in the Ṛig-vēda, his association with Indra. Yet it is a very clearly marked trait in his character. Not only do the poets often couple the two gods in prayer and praise, but they often tell us that the one performed his characteristic deeds with the help of the other. They say that Vishṇu made his three strides by the power of Indra (VIII. xii. 27), or for the sake of Indra (Vāl. iv. 3), and even that Indra strode along with Vishṇu (VI. lxix. 5, VII. xix. 6), and on the other hand they tell us often that it was by the aid of Vishṇu that Indra overcame Vṛitra and other malignant foes. "Friend Vishṇu, stride out lustily," cries Indra before he can strike down Vṛitra (IV. xviii. 11).[14] The answer to this riddle I find in the Brāhmaṇas, the priestly literature which is about to follow immediately after the Vēda. In plain unequivocal words, the Brāhmaṇas tell us again and again that _Vishṇu is the sacrifice_.[15] When they repeat this they are repeating an old hieratic tradition, and it is one that perfectly explains the facts of the case. Vishṇu, I conceive, was originally nothing more or less than the embodied spirit of the sacrificial rites. His name seems to be derived from the root _vish_, meaning stimulation or inspiration; and this is exactly what the sacrifice is supposed in priestly theory to do. The sacrifice, accompanied by prayer and praise, is imagined to have a magic power of its own, by which the gods worshipped in it are strengthened to perform their divine functions. One poet says to Indra: "When thy two wandering Bays thou dravest hither, thy praiser laid within thine arms the thunder" (RV. I. lxiii. 2); and still, more boldly another says: "Sacrifice, Indra, made thee wax so mighty ... worship helped thy bolt when slaying the dragon" (III. xxxii. 12). So it would be very natural for the priests to conceive this spirit of the sacrificial rites as a personal deity; and this deity, the Brāhmaṇas assure us, is Vishṇu. Then the idea of the three strides and the association with Indra would easily grow up in the priestly imagination. The inspiring power of the sacrifice is supposed to pervade the three realms of the universe, earth, sky, and upper heavens; this idea is expressed in the common ritual formula _bhūr bhavas svaḥ_and is symbolized by three steps taken by the priest in certain ceremonies, which are translated into the language of myth as the three strides of Vishṇu.[16] Observe that in the Ṛig-vēda the upper heaven is not the dwelling-place of Vishṇu only; Agni the Fire-god, Indra, and Sōma have their home in it also (RV. I. clip. 6, IV. xxvi. 6, xxvii. 3-4, V. iii. 3, VIII. lxxxix. 8, IX. lxiii. 27, lxvi. 30, lxviii. 6, lxxvii. 2, lxxxvi. 24, X. i. 3, xi. 4, xix. 8, cxliv. 4). Later, however, when their adventitious divinity begins to fade away from Agni and Sōma, and Indra is allotted a special paradise of his own, this "highest step" will be regarded as peculiar to Vishṇu, _Vishṇōḥ paramam padam_.

As soon as this spirit of sacrifice was thus personified, he at once attached himself to Indra; for Indra is pre-eminently the god of action, and for his activities, he needs to be stimulated by sacrifice and praise. As the priests will tell us in plain unvarnished words, "he to whom the Sacrifice comes as portion slays Indra" (AB. I. iv.). Therefore we are told that Vishṇu aids Indra in his heroic exploits, that Vishṇu takes his strides and presses Sōmaso that Indra may be strengthened for his tasks. Now we can see the full meaning of Indra's cry before striking Vṛitra, "Friend Vishṇu, stride out lustily!"; for until the sacrifice has put forth its mystic energy the god cannot strike his blow. We are told also that Vishṇu cooks buffaloes and boils milk for Indra,[17] for buffaloes were no doubt anciently offered to Indra. The vivid reality of Indra's character has clothed Vishṇu with some of its flesh and blood; originally a priestly abstraction, he has become through association with Indra a living being, a real god. The blood which has thus been poured into his veins will enable him to live through a critical period of his life until by combination with another deity he will rise to new and supreme sovereignty. But of that more anon. Meanwhile, let us note the significance of this union of Vishṇu and Indra in the Vēda. Vishṇu, the spirit of Sacrifice, is in a sense representative of the Brahman priesthood, and Indra, as I have shown, is commonly regarded as typical of the warrior order. In the Ṛig-vēda Indra is powerless without Vishṇu's mystic service, and Vishṇu labors to aid Indra in his heroic works for the welfare of men and gods. Surely this is an allegory, though the priests may so far be only dimly conscious of its full meaning--an allegory bodying forth the priestly ideal of the reign of righteousness, in which the King is strong by the mystic power of the Priest, and the Priest lives for the service of the King.

There is another god who is destined to become in future ages Vishṇu's chief rival--Rudra, "The Tawny," or Śiva, "The Gracious." He belongs to the realm of popular superstition, a spiteful demon ready to smite men and cattle with the disease but dispensing healing balms and medicines to those who win his favor. The Ṛigvēdic priests as yet do not take much interest in him, and for the most part, they leave him to their somewhat despised kinsmen the Atharvans, who do a thriving trade in hymns and spells to secure the common folk against his wrath.

There are many more gods, godlings, and spirits in the Vēdic religion; but we must pass over them. We have seen enough, I hope, to give us a fair idea of the nature and value of that religion in general. What then is its value?

The Ṛigvēda is essentially a priestly book, but it is not entirely a priestly book. Much of the thought to which it gives utterance is popular in origin and sentiment and is by no means of the lowest order. On this groundwork, the priests have built up a system of hieratic thought and ritual of their own, in which there is much that deserves a certain respect. There is a good deal of fine poetry in it. There is also in it some idea of a law of righteousness: despite much wild and unmoral myth and fancy, its gods for the most part are not capricious demons but spirits who act by established laws, majestic and wise beings who have embodied the highest ideals to which men have risen as yet. Moreover, the priests in the later books have given us some mystic hymns containing vigorous and pregnant speculations on the deepest questions of existence, speculations which are indeed fanciful and unscientific, but which nevertheless have in them the germs of the powerful idealism that is destined to arise in centuries to come. On the other hand, the priests have cast their system in the mold of ritualism. Ritual, ceremony, sacrifice, and professional benefit--are their predominant interests. The priestly ceremonies are conceived to possess a magical power of their own; and, indexed laws of ritual by which these ceremonies are regulated tend to eclipse, and finally even swallow up, the laws of moral righteousness under which the gods live. A few generations more, and the priesthood will frankly announce its ritual to be the supreme law of the universe. Meanwhile the, ey are becoming more and more indifferent to the personalities of the gods when they have preserved any; they are quite ready to ascribe attributes of one deity to another, even attributes of nominal supremacy, with unscrupulous inconsistency and dubious sincerity; for the personalities of the different gods are beginning to fade away in their eyes, and in their mind is arising the conception of a single universal Godhead.

www.ingramcontent.com/pod-product-compliance
Lightning Source LLC
Chambersburg PA
CBHW031639170726

47990CB00018B/1566